The Choices

YOU

Make Affect

Others

By Dana Monroe

Natarielle Writes LLC, Publishing House
4431 Augusta Road Suite 7382
Savannah, Georgia 31408

Printed in the United States of America

For information on bulk purchases or author speaking engagements, please contact Natarielle Writes LLC at info@natariellethebookdoctor.com

ISBN- 9798439293902

I dedicate this book to the following people: my Lord and Savior, Jesus Christ, my mother, my siblings, my husband, my children, my late grandparents and cousin who I called grandmother (Evangelist Geraldine Burroughs), my late pastor (Elder Terry), my church family, my supportive and praying friends, and my readers. May God bless you for reading this book. May you be encouraged to put God first in your decision-making in life.

Proverbs 3:5-6 is one of my favorite scriptures. It reminds us to trust in the Lord with all thine heart and lean not unto thine own understanding. In all thy ways acknowledge him, and he shall direct your paths.

Special thanks to my publisher,

Natarielle, The Book Doctor, for her encouragement and prayers

Table of Contents

Introduction

In life, we have to make choices every day: to get up or not, to go to work or not, what to wear, etc. The choices you make will affect your day, your life and others that you are responsible for like your children, wife or husband. The Bible is a good book to help you make good choices and to show what will happen when you make bad choices in life. I believe that the Bible was written as a road map to guide us. There is one scripture that I have carried with me since 2013. That is Proverbs 3:5-6, and it states, "Trust in the Lord with all thine heart and lean not unto thine own understanding. In all thy ways acknowledge him and he shall direct thy paths." This scripture will help you to make good choices. All we have to do is seek God first before we make decisions. If we lean on our own understanding and way of thinking, sometimes we won't make a good choice. And sometimes we don't see the lesson until it's too late.

I am going to compare choices that we make from the Bible's point of view and my life's point of view. One of the persons that I would like to use for an example is King David. The Lord chose David to be king after Saul kept being disobedient. The Lord rejected Saul and honored David.

David was the youngest out of his brothers, and he was keeping sheep. He was ruddy with a beautiful countenance and goodly to look upon. The Lord told Samuel to arise and anoint him in the midst of his brethren, and the Spirit of the Lord came upon David from that day forward.

Throughout David's life, the Lord was with him while he was keeping the sheep, fighting a lion and a bear. David stood up and slayed Goliath. David had prayed to God first for answers after encouraging and strengthening himself when he was coming back from battle. He saw his camp burned down. All of his family and his soldiers' families were gone. The other soldiers were talking about stoning David. The Lord answered David to pursue the enemies, for you will certainly overtake them and rescue the captives. So, the choices we make do affect others. When we seek God first, and he directs us, all we have to do is obey him.

David also made some bad choices in life like the great sin with Bathsheba and having her husband killed while in battle. The prophet, Nathan, spoke to King David with these words: the Lord says, the sword shall never depart from your house because you have despised me and have taken the wife of Uriah the Hittite to be your wife. In spite all of this David repented and continued to serve the Lord. Moreover, the Lord continued to be with David and blessed him with a son named Solomon. *The choices we make do affect others.* All we have to do is seek God first to make good choices in life. When we make bad choices, we can't give up; just get back up and seek God for help. Do your best to correct the mistake and continue to serve God.

I made some good choices in life, and I made some bad choices too, but one thing I learned is that the Lord is still with you. I learned when you feel like giving up, the Lord is there to lift you up. Be encouraged, and let the Lord lead you and guide you to make good choices.

THE
CHOICES
YOU
MAKE
AFFECT
OTHERS

Living in the North

The first thing that I remember as a child is living in New York riding my bike. My grandfather, my brother and I were in the backyard, and my grandfather was showing us how to ride our bikes. I also remember my brother and I walking to school. The school was just a few blocks from where my grandparents lived. At the time, we were living with them.

My brother and I were a few months apart. He was born a few months earlier than expected, so I am the oldest. My birthday is in September, and his birthday is in June. Between those months, we are the same age. We had a lot of people thinking we were twins.

My grandparents lived in the suburbs, and they had a big house with a basement and an attic. My brother and I slept in the attic of the house. One night, my brother was very mad about something, but he wouldn't tell me what it was. I kept asking him what was bothering him, but he would not tell me. The next thing I knew, my grandmother was saying we burned down her house! Since my grandparents' house burned down, they moved to South Carolina. They were living on their own land, and they started a farm.

After that, we moved to different parts of New York. I remember going to different schools. I hated it because I would get used to the teachers, make friends and then we would have to move again. It was hard.

My brother and I would make up games to play. We would find a curtain rod and a big box. We attached the curtain rod to the box to pull the person inside the box around the house. My brother was holding the rod and cut his finger and had to get stitches. Then I was outside playing with no shoes on and got broken pieces of glass in the bottom of my feet. I had to have the pieces of glass taken out.

My father drank a lot. He would come home very late at night and get in fights with my mother. My brother was angry about this, and I was too. I was scared and angry at the same time. When our father began to get loud, we would just stay in our room and be quiet. His loud noises always woke us up. Fear kept us awake during those times, but we had no idea that that same fear would bring about such great changes in our lives.

THE
CHOICES
YOU
MAKE
AFFECT
OTHERS

Heading Down South

One day my brother and I were running, jumping from cabin to cabin on the train. We were moving from New York to Georgia. It was a big change, staying with my mother's cousin in this tiny house for almost a year. At the end of the year we moved to South Carolina in an area called Wagon Branch. It was the country! In the area where we lived, we had to drive eight miles to get to the actual town and go to the grocery store. We also had to ride a bus to school, and the children were very mean. They always wanted to fight my brother and me.

My brother had to teach me how to fight. He said that he was tired of me getting beat up by the other children. After he taught me how to fight, I knew how to protect myself and help my brother out when the children wanted to fight him.

I realized growing up that my parents always got the news that my brother, Eddie, and I had been to the principal's office. I found out that we had family working at the school: aunts and cousins working as teachers or kitchen cooks. My parents knew what was going on with us before we even got home to tell them ourselves.

My brother and I both stayed in the principal's office, and he knew our names very well. He would even call out our full names. He would say, "Dana Renee Gibson, you are back in here again!" I would not say anything because I knew he would hit me with the tiny strap or the big wooden paddle that he kept in his office.

One day I got smart and wore a pair of shorts under my skirt. I was good and padded down. I went to the principal's office, and I turned around to submit to the beating. The principal asked, "Don't you want to plead your case about why you are in here?" I said that I did not want to plead my case. I knew that I would still get punished. After my paddling, I went back to class. From that day on, I would wear extra clothes to school, just in case I got paddled.

One day, the school bus that I was riding was racing the school bus next to us on the road. During that time, the school board allowed teenagers to drive the school buses. My bus driver blacked out and we ran headfirst into a big tree. One person got thrown out of the front window of the bus. My brother and I were sitting in the middle of the bus and were thrown to the front of the bus. Some of us went to the hospital. I hurt my right knee (it was swollen), and my brother hurt his stomach. Our parents and the parents of the other children were mad that the teenagers were racing with the bus, but after a few months, everything was okay.

Kinfolk and Church Folk

In the next year, I was in eighth grade, and I would be at the high school. After three years of fighting, I finally moved up to being a teenager. No more fighting. Now the boys were liking me. A few wanted to be my boyfriend, but there was one in particular that I was sweet on. His name was Anthony. He asked me out to the homecoming game, and he came by my house. My father answered the door and said, "Hey, cousin! You came to take your cousin to the game?" Anthony and I were both very sad. And the next thing I knew Anthony went back home to Florida.

During one of my visits to my grandmother's house, my aunt came over and was talking to her mother (my grandmother) about going back to New York because my grandmother told her that we were most likely kin to everyone out here in South Carolina. Then, I thought about Anthony and me, and I didn't want to talk to any of the boys in South Carolina. I decided to just focus on my family and my artwork, specifically drawing.

I always loved spending time with my grandfather. When he came to visit, we had such fun. Grandpa was so funny, and he always brought us candy or gave us money. I enjoyed going to spend time at my grandparent's house. They lived on a large property with chickens, pigs, and a big field with a lot of cucumbers, watermelon, and field peas.

One day, my grandfather told me to go feed the chickens. I was so scared that I dropped the food and left the gate open. My grandfather was furious! After that, he never let me feed the chickens again. But I was okay with that. As long as I could spend time with my grandfather, I didn't care if it was fishing or being on the farm.

Sunday Service

Church was always a strong part of our lives. My grandmother loved church, and she would take my mother, my siblings and me to church. I would also go with my grandmother to help clean the church, and we would sing in the choir on Sunday. We would also help serve food in the kitchen for special occasions. From the age of nine, I was at all of the church anniversaries, Bible study, revivals and any other church meeting.

One Sunday, I was sitting across from my grandpa, mocking the pastor on everything he was saying. When he said yeah, I said yeah. When he said glory, I said glory, but the last time I said something, he didn't say anything. It was just me, and I was loud. I said Yeah! Yeah! The whole church was looking at me. My grandmother was sitting up front with the other leaders of the church, and she gave me a look that put fear in me. My grandfather was sitting with the deacons of the church, and he came and got me. He took me outside, and he talked to me. He said, "You know your grandmother is gonna get you!" And then he started laughing! I wasn't expecting that. Next, my grandmother came walking around the church, and she started fussing. But she couldn't stay mad too long because we all started laughing. I thought sure that I was going to get a beating. The Lord spared me that day. Yeah!

Another Sunday afternoon, my grandparents came to our house to pay us a visit. My siblings and I were in the backyard playing church. I was the pastor, of course. I was mocking the way the pastor preached, and my grandmother caught me. She got on me about that, and the next Sunday she had my siblings and me at the front of the church singing. That's how we became the Gibson Family Singing Group.

For several years we sang at our church and other churches. At first I hated it because I felt like I sounded terrible. With a lot of practice, we began to sound alright. To this day, my siblings and I sing and have nice voices. I raised my children to sing, and my children can play the drums and the keyboard. Most of all, we serve the Lord.

THE
CHOICES
YOU
MAKE
AFFECT
OTHERS

Losing my Father

A few years had passed, and my father continued to drink. He would come home and fight my mother. At this time I was about 11 years old, and I tried to help my mother by fighting my dad off of her. He threatened to beat me, so I went back to my room and just looked out the window. I said to myself, *when I get married I will not marry someone who will drink and smoke and hit on me.* The moon was so big and bright that night. I stared at it until I fell asleep. I didn't remember until I became a grown woman, and the Lord brought it back to my mind. Several years later, I met a wonderful man, and we have been married for over 30 years now. He doesn't smoke or drink or hit me.

One night I had a dream about my father dying. I did not tell anyone about the dream. My father came home late one night and woke everyone in the house up. He said who was dreaming about me? I didn't say a word, but he looked at me. He could tell that it was me. He went into his room and became very sick. I had to go to my aunt's house to get her to call for help for my dad. They took him to the hospital, and a few days later he died. That was the worst day of my life.

I loved my father. I was 12 years old when he passed away, and after that my life changed forever. I got to see how people truly fight over material possessions. They fought over my father's car and other things. My mother wasn't in any shape to make any decisions. There were six of us kids, and I was the oldest.

Shortly after my father's passing we moved back to Georgia. I hated moving, and I was MAD! But I didn't say a word to anyone. I held the anger inside of me.

We were all cramped together in a two-bedroom house with only one bathroom for nine people. Oh yeah, and this is when I found out that we had an older brother. He couldn't stand us and didn't want us there in the house. He would say mean things to us. Life was hard.

During this time we also had to walk to school. I told myself that I wasn't going to be around anyone in the neighborhood, and for four years I kept my promise to myself.

After living in the cramped house for two years, my mother, my siblings and I moved into a much bigger house. We had two bathrooms and five bedrooms, plenty of space. Things were starting to get better for us, except for the fact that my older brother was still mean and hateful.

Although I didn't care for many people, I started to form a close relationship with my mother's cousin. I asked her if I could call her grandmother, even though she wasn't old enough to be my grandmother. She agreed. Before we begin to form a bond, I was full of anger. There was so much that had built up inside of me, and talking to her made me feel better.

My mother didn't talk much, but she made sure that we were fed and that we had clean clothes to wear. She didn't talk about her upbringing or her family. My cousin/grandmother told me the things that I needed to know as I got older. She told me that my mother's father, mother, siblings, and grandparents all died in a house fire.

She was the only survivor, and she was 13 years old at the time. I cried when I learned of this news. It made me understand why my mother wanted my siblings and I to be so close by her side. She spoiled us and tried to give us the world. To this day, she does the same thing. As I write this book, she is 77 years old and still has a heart of gold.

The Power of Prayer

My family believed in going to the doctor, but we also believed in the power of prayer. As a teenage girl, I suffered with earaches. One day when my grandmother took me to the doctor, he said that I had a buildup of fluid in my ears. He gave me some medicine, and it took a week before I felt any relief. After I got a little better, I started having problems in the other ear. This time we didn't go to the doctor. My grandmother took me to church, and when they called for the prayer line, I went up for prayer.

After church we went back home, and I didn't even think about my ear bothering me until late that night. I said, "Wow, the pain is gone. The swelling is gone too!" I thought about this thing for quite a while. It took more than a week for me to feel better when I went to the doctor and got medicine. When I went to church with the same problem and got prayed for, I received my healing right then. Who would you serve, man or God? I am like Joshua: as for me and my house, we will serve the Lord!

After that experience I wanted to be saved. I was faithful going to church, cleaning the church, helping to serve food, singing in the choir, and assisting the Sunday school teachers with the youth day programs. I was 18 years old at the time.

The Aftermath of Death

After I graduated from high school, I started going to Savannah Vo-Tech. That's what we called it then. Now it's called Savannah Technical College. My cousin/grandmother would take me to school each day. I would always say see you later, and she would say okay, see you soon. We would both say bye. But one morning when she was dropping me off, I said see you later and she didn't say anything. She just had a sad look on her face. That bothered me the entire day. I kept thinking about it.

That afternoon my name was called to the front office. My pastor was there standing in the office, and I was scared because he never came to pick me up from school. I would only see him at church. I knew that he had some bad news. He gave me a hug and told me that my cousin/grandmother had died.

I couldn't believe it. I was shocked, and I felt like my whole world crashed before me. I had to change again for the worst. I was thinking *WHY*?!

My grandmother went back home and died. All of my siblings were home, and my mother was all upset. I can only imagine how she felt. The whole situation was very upsetting and very sad for everyone. I don't like when someone dies and family members come over and start going through your clothes and begin to take things. They also come over and want to take charge, planning things knowing that they are not even going to pay for them or help you after the funeral. This makes me mad.

My grandmother had a lot of patience with me. After the death of my father, she helped me to get my life together. She showed me how to pay bills, cook, clean, and take care of the house. She taught me how to pray and fast. I was truly hurt that she left me so soon.

I would have dreams, and she would tell me to pray and ask God what they meant. One thing she told me was that I was not going to die until my work was finished. I was so afraid of dying because my father died at age 32. Now she had left me at the age of 46, and my sister died at the age of 16.

Well, I had to really get myself together. I couldn't break down even if I wanted to. My mother was a mess, and my siblings were really confused. I had to step up to the plate and be in charge. For a while, it was going well, and then my siblings began to act out, being grown. I couldn't control them. My mother started stepping up and helping, but they weren't listening to her either.

When I was around 21 years old, my father's parents came to visit. I told my grandmother (my father's mother) that I wanted to go back to New York and finish school up there. My aunt, Helena, told me that there was a school that I could finish my classes out there and I could stay with her, but my mother cried because she didn't want me to go. So, I stayed, fighting with my siblings and trying to keep the house together.

I met this guy and married him for the wrong reasons, just to get away from what was going on at home. What a bad choice I made! It took a year to get out of that mess. I had to ask for forgiveness and repent to God for what I had done. Please don't get married unless the Lord tells you to and because you love the person. All that time, I only thought about myself. Then, I realized that my choice affected my whole family. What a price to pay for that one bad choice!

After going through that ordeal, I moved back home for a while. My sister next to me and I were together one day talking. She said, "When it's time for you to die, it's just time for you to die." I said, "No, some people make themselves die before their time, but let's change the subject."

Later that day, my sister took sick and had to go in the hospital. Early one morning a few days later, the doctor told us to get to the hospital soon. When we got there they were putting a sheet over my sister. They told me what was going on, and I passed out. When I woke up I was in this little room crying. Here I am again, angry and upset with my family members trying to take over. And my mother is upset all over again.

I ended up having to tell my grandmother and my aunt off. At the funeral home while we were planning the service for my sister, I told the director that there would be no viewing at the end. Then, when it was time for the end of the service, the funeral home officials came to open the coffin. I stood up and said, "We said no viewing!" They told me that my aunt changed it. I was so heated that the pastor had to come calm me down.

No one was there to help me with my mother after everything was over. Life was hard after this, but with God we made it through.

THE
CHOICES
YOU
MAKE
AFFECT
OTHERS

Seeing Double

S ome time later, I got married again. This time it was
because I was in love, and I asked God to teach me
how to be a wife and a mother. God showed me,
guided me, and helped me to do just what I asked. He taught
me how to listen and make the right choices.

The Lord sent my husband's cousin to tell us about a
program where an organization was building homes in
Effingham. I asked her where Effingham was and if she
would get the information for us. I wanted to look into the
program.

My husband's cousin came back to check and see if we
heard anything about the house. I told her no. She was

working to get into the same program and had heard back from the organization.

A few days later, my husband and I got a letter that we were accepted! We had to come to the office and submit the rest of the paperwork. The Lord blessed us with our first house in Effingham. We weren't even thinking or looking for a house and didn't know anything about Effingham, but the Lord worked everything out for us.

After moving to Effingham, I asked the Lord for a son and talked to my husband about it as well. At first, my husband wasn't sure about having more children. We already had two girls, for some reason, I wanted a son. The Lord blessed. At three months, the doctor was measuring me, and he said, "I'm getting that you are much further along than you are saying." The doctor said he would send me for an ultrasound.

Some time passed, and I went to get the ultrasound done. Beforehand, my mother-in-law said that I was going to have twins. I told her not to say that, but I'd forgotten about her prophecy.

I was excited and nervous at the same time about the ultrasound. The nurse technician came in and was about to start the procedure. She began to place the instrument on my stomach, but she got called away and had to step out. I happened to look at the monitor screen and started to scream. The nurse came running in asking, "Are you okay, Mrs. Monroe?" I said, "I see two heads!" The nurse told me to calm down so she could check. "Aww, Mrs. Monroe, you are having twins! It's a little early to tell what they are, but there's Baby A, and there's Baby B. She gave me a picture to take with me.

At that time, the statement my mother-in-law made came back to me. I went to her house, and my father-in-law was there too. I told them the news, and they were excited. My husband came to their house. I was waiting for him there, but my mother-in-law beat me to telling him. He was standing in the doorway doing a Fred Sanford act by holding his heart (lol).

At work there were about three ladies expecting babies at the same time. One lady was having one baby, I was having twins, and another lady was having triplets! So, the manager said I'm not drinking the water in here (lol, smh)!

A few weeks later I hit my four-month mark of pregnancy. I was at home with my two-year-old, and I began to feel some pain. I got her and told her, "You have to be still for Mommy, and we both have to lie in bed until Daddy comes home." Bless the Lord that he came home early, and we went straight to the hospital after dropping the children off at my mother's house. When we got to the hospital, the doctor checked me out and said there was nothing he could do. He told me that the babies weighed less than 1 pound, and he left out the room. I told my husband to come to me and pray. So, we prayed, and the pain stopped. When the doctor came back in, I told him that the pain had stopped. He listened to me, but he still needed to check to be sure everything was alright. He left for a while and came back to check me again, and he said everything looks good. My God is an awesome God!

After that the doctor put me on bed rest. I could not work anymore. From that time on, I laid my hands on my stomach and prayed over my babies.

Now, I had more doctors visits than usual because I was carrying twins, and I was a high-risk patient. The next news I got was that one of my babies' organs were not developing properly. But I continued to pray.

I had several ultrasounds, and they finally told me the sex of the baby. One was a girl, but they couldn't tell the sex of the other baby because his legs were together. The nurse tried to get the baby to move, but the baby would not budge. So it took another month or two before I finally found out that the other baby was a boy. The doctors still gave me the same news about his organs, but I continued to pray every day over my babies.

My aunt (my father's sister) in New York had a twin girl and boy just a year before I gave birth to my twins. This trait definitely runs in my family.

In my eighth month of pregnancy, I got sick and had to go to the hospital. They told me that I had either the flu or pneumonia. I was very sick. The doctors had to check my twins to make sure they did not have the virus also. I stayed in the hospital for several weeks, and everything turned out okay! What an awesome God we serve!

I came back to the hospital early because the doctor wanted me to go ahead and have the babies three weeks before my due date. They were still saying that my son would not make it and that both babies would be underweight, but I kept praying.

When my babies were born, the girl weighed 6 pounds and 11 ounces, and she was 22 inches long. My son weighed 5 pounds and 5 ounces, and he was also 22 inches long. They were born seven minutes apart, and nothing was wrong with my babies. They were both healthy. We serve an awesome God!

Favor Ain't Fair

The Lord blessed me and guided me on how to raise my children. He also favored me on my job. After being there only a week, I was promoted to assistant manager. After one month, I was offered a manager position.

At that time, my twins were old enough to go to Head Start. I cried when I had to leave them on their first day. When I had time, I would volunteer at Head Start. When a job became available as a teachers aide, I applied. The Lord moved on my behalf with favor over my life, and I got the job. The Lord blessed me to get the experience that I needed while I work there, so I got to teach and be with my children. What an awesome God!

During the years working there I learned a lot. I was getting a spiritual and a natural education. On my first day as an employee, I met with the head administrator. I originally met with her assistant who hired me when she really wasn't supposed to. All I did was put in the application, and the Lord fixed it so that my calls went through, even though the assistant said she did not want any phone calls. My calls went through every single time. Then, she asked me to come meet with her, and I did. She asked only one question: tell me something about yourself? I did just that, and she said, "You are hired!"

I went back to the school, and I caught some of the employees gathered together talking about me. I listened for a minute and then went back to my classroom. I was hurt, but I was also excited about what God did for me. The head administrator called me to meet with her the next day, and I was a little nervous. The Spirit told me to go, take my papers with me, be calm, and make sure you look directly at her. So I did just that, and her spirit calmed down right before my eyes. She told me that her assistant who hired me was supposed to have me go through a hiring process, but it was okay. I was hired, and she released me to go back to work. My God is awesome!

The ladies on the job couldn't believe it. My God had me there for a reason. I learned so much and received spiritual elevation. My self-esteem improved also. I didn't love myself prior to this time in my life. My self-esteem was very low, and the Lord had the children there to keep coming to me and saying I love you. They would give me hugs all day, especially the day that I had this particular interview. The other teachers were looking and watching me even while we were on the playground. Different ones would come up and hug me and say I love you. I began to feel happy and my spirit lifted up.

I left from work that day and went to the store. At the store, a person came up to me and said, "Can I hug you? The Lord told me to tell you that he loves you and to give you a hug." Then, several more people in different places said the exact same thing. The Lord will build you up and give you strength in the time when you need it. We serve an awesome God!

Throughout my seven years working at the school, my God was sooooo good to me. When I left there, the Lord blessed me to open up a daycare center of my own. I was scared, and I waited a whole year before I moved on what the Lord said to me. But when I finally moved, that same day the Lord put me with the right person. I had all of the information and the right person to help me set up the same day! What an awesome God we serve!

My business was amazing! I thank God for favor over my life. I thank God for placing love in my life. I can now show love to people who hated me. I don't show hatred anymore, and I'm certainly not trying to get even with anyone because of how they treated me. I thank God for changing me.

Growing up I really don't remember the good in my childhood. It seems like I only remember the hurtful things. I had anger and fighting inside of me, and also some fear. I had a fear of dying, getting close to people and loving them because I thought they would die and leave me. So, I kept a distance from people so I would not get hurt. But my God helped me with all of that. Now I can love, and I have gotten over the fear of dying if I reach a certain age. My father was 32 when he died, and my grandmother was 46 when she died. I am way past those ages now. God is awesome! Now I have four grandchildren, and my four children are all grown up.

They have all graduated from high school, and the twins are in college. What an awesome God!

While raising my children, I kept them close to me. I made sure they were in church, and we had family vacations every year.

THE
CHOICES
YOU
MAKE
AFFECT
OTHERS

My Husband's Miracle

I love my children and my husband, and I took my vow as a wife (in sickness and in health) seriously. My husband was a long distance truck driver, and I would always pray to the Lord to keep and protect him on the road. He had several accidents where the truck was totaled, but my husband came out without a scratch. What an awesome God!

On one occasion when my husband was coming back from a long distance trip, he parked his truck and called me at 4 A.M. to come pick him up. He said he wasn't feeling well and couldn't drive anymore. I went to get him, and he was burning up with a fever. I had to help him out of the truck. I got him into the car, went home and got the kids and dropped them off to my mom's house before we went to the hospital. My husband was admitted for the flu/pneumonia. The next day, the doctor said they were going to let him go home because he was doing well. I left to go get clothes for him and to check on the children. When I got back, my husband had slipped into a coma! He had a sickle cell crisis. I was thinking to myself *what in the world happened?* I started to blame myself thinking that I should not have left him.

Later on the doctors came and talked to me. They explained everything and said there was nothing else that they could do, but they would try to keep my husband comfortable.

That night, I sat by the window in the hospital room. The room was dark, and only the bathroom light was on. The door was cracked just a little. I heard a voice quoting the words from Psalm 121 to me. The voice said to me he shall live and not die. Then, I felt a breeze pass by me in the area where I was sitting. My spirit was lifted, and I was excited! Then I asked, "Monroe how do you feel?" My husband responded, "I am okay." I rejoiced in the room that night!

The next day, doctors came one by one to see him, and they couldn't believe it. They all said he wouldn't live, but my God said he shall live and not die. What an awesome God! That next year, on the same date, he was back in the hospital. My husband got sick again, but my God was with us, and the angels were guarding us at the hospital. My husband's friend came and told me I needed to go home and get some rest. I said, "I am not leaving him." But my feet were swollen and my feelings came over me just like the last time when I left to get clothes for him to go home and came back and he was in a coma. So, I did not want to leave him, but my husband's friend convinced me to go home and rest. He said that he would let me know if anything changed that night.

I couldn't rest. I just sat by the window praying, but that night they gave my husband some blood, and he woke up asking for me. The next day I went back to the hospital, and my husband was doing well. Then, it was time for us to go home on the same date that he left last year. But this time, it leapt in my spirit, and I spoke that we are not coming back here again. The Lord blessed us, and to this day we have not gone back to the hospital. What an awesome God!

As time passed, my family and I enjoyed and visited many churches. My heart wasn't in many of the churches we visited and joined, but I did it because I felt like we needed a church home. My husband wasn't ready to start on his own church. Also, a part of me was scared, but at the same time I wanted to do the right thing. I learned that the choices you make do affect others. I learned this later in life.

Throughout the years, I sat back and wondered why this and that happened. When you look back over your life and you make choices and you only think about yourself, you realize that in some situations you didn't want the responsibility or you were scared to mess up. Many excuses come to your mind. But now I realize if I only took the time to get by myself, pray and ask for help from the Lord, he would guide me through as he did all the other times in my life. I wouldn't have fear and second-guessing myself, or look for others to help me. I learned that it's important to look to the Lord because he is the one who all my help comes from. I learned to never stop praying and spending time with the Lord. You may not notice it at the moment, but people are depending on you and may even be following you.

Going Through my

Medical Storm

I stayed at a church where the people were treating me so bad, but it seemed like my family members enjoyed themselves. I felt like *where else can I go?* I had been hurt, and I didn't trust leaders anymore. But then things started happening. I fell sick, and my family had many financial problems all at once.

One Friday evening I was closing up my daycare center, and I made it home to sit down on the couch and put my legs up. I looked at my legs and both of them were red and swollen. I stayed there on the couch for several hours before

I moved to the bedroom. On Saturday, I didn't do anything. On Sunday morning, I got up to go to the bathroom and get ready for church. I was out of breath and felt so tired. So I prayed, *Lord give me strength to do praise and worship*.

I barely made it to the car and into the church. I went up to the front of the church to do praise and worship. I was fine while I was singing, but afterwards my back hurt, I felt tired, and I could hardly breathe. When the guest speaker asked if anyone needed prayer, I went up for prayer and nothing happened. When I went back home I felt the same way. I prayed for strength to work on Monday and Tuesday, and the Lord blessed.

On Wednesday during nap time, I was taking a nap with the children. My daughter called, and I woke up to talk to her.

"Mom, how are you doing today?" My daughter was concerned.

"About the same," I answered.

"I am coming to take you to the hospital."

"Okay," I responded.

Well, my daughter and I went to the hospital and the nurse asked what was wrong with me, but she didn't do anything. She just told me to come back in a few days. My daughter was so upset that we left and went to another hospital in Savannah. While my daughter was signing me in, a nurse looked at me and said, "You look pale, ma'am." She took me straight into the back, and the next thing I remember I was in a room with several people standing over me. A lady with a white coat on was saying, "You're supposed to be dead!" She repeated this several times to me, but God did it!

The doctor put me in ICU. While I was in there, I looked around, and a nurse was hooking up blood to give to me. My spirit said, "The Blood of Jesus" when each pint was being placed. The doctor gave orders for me not to be moved because I had a blood clot lodged in my right lung. I needed blood because my own blood count was so low.

The doctors were trying to figure out what to fix because I had several problems going on in my body. Nobody knew what to do, but my God was with me. He did not allow fear to enter me. I kept looking to him and reciting the 121st Psalm which stayed with me. This is the psalm that the Spirit spoke to me when my husband was in the hospital. My daughter bought a CD to the hospital with a song by Donald Lawrence that really touched my spirit. The song, *Live and not Die*, gave me great encouragement.

The doctors later came in with a plan, and I was in the hospital for about two weeks, even during my birthday. I had to come back in six months for surgery.

I'm reminded of another time on August 27, 2007 when I was in the hospital. My current hospital stay is on today's date, August 28, 2021. It is 2 o'clock in the morning as I am writing this. How awesome is our God that he would remind me of this!

On the first day that I was in ICU, I rang the bell because I needed to use the bathroom. My nurse never introduced herself, and she never came to help me. A nurse down the hall came to check on me and to talk with me. I was telling her about what the Lord said, and she said she would check on me while she was working. The nurse who was assigned to me was standing by the window talking to another male nurse about me, saying all kinds of mean things. I thank God for giving me a new nurse. I told my doctor about her and that the nurse down the hall was very helpful to me. Then it came to my spirit to pray, *Lord please don t let anyone in my room who does not mean me any good.* And the Lord answered my prayer.

When you are going through something in your life, it needs to be just you and the Lord. You don't need a room full of doubters, gossipers, or nosy people pulling your spirit down. You don't need to have to fight all the spirits trying to attach themselves to you. This is the time you need to spend with God to listen and obey him. Plead the blood of Jesus over everything: your doctors, nurses and even the blood that is given to you. You have to pray in order to make sure you are given the right care that you need.

While I was in the hospital, I was praying for others who were in the hospital as well. Also, while I was in ICU, I kept hearing bells going off and people were running down the hallway. Men in suits were rolling someone on a gurney. At that time, a little fear tried to come over me. So, I started saying the blood of Jesus! I put my mind on something else. Thankfully, one of my church members was a CNA, and she would stop by my room to visit. When she got off of her shift that night and we talked, at first we were both scared.

We continued to talk about the goodness of the Lord, and then I started feeling better.

After a few days in ICU, I was moved to a regular room, but I still could not get around by myself. So, I asked for extra pillows and the person who was fixing my room gave me used pillows. I laid my head on those pillows and began to feel sick. I removed the pillows and threw them across the room. I asked the nurse for new pillows, and she brought them to me. This time I made sure I saw the plastic come off of them so I would know that they were new.

It was at this time that I realized that you really need to have God with you at all times. I didn't just talk about God in church, but in the hospital, I was praying and asking God to watch over me and be my nurse, doctor, lab tech, food preparer, and my everything. If you are not on top of your sickness, you will be stressed out and depressed without Jesus being there with you and in your heart to guide you through it. I learned a lot through prayer and meditation. Listening to gospel music also helped me. I know for sure where I would be without Jesus there guiding and helping me: I would be scared with the doctor standing over me saying, "You were supposed to be dead over three times!"

That is what the doctor was saying while I was looking up at her on the hospital bed. She said that I would be put in ICU because I could not move at all. There was a large blood clot in my right lung. That was enough for me. But my awesome God touched me right there; he reminded me, strengthened me, encouraged me, and took the fear away. He took over.

When I finally went home I continued to get better. While I was going through this, my babies (the twins) were in their senior year of high school. I am so very thankful for the Head Start teacher who came to help take care of my daycare business while I was in the hospital. She did an awesome job! God also favored me. He lead a doctor at the hospital take over my case and paid for the doctor's visit and the surgery. During the six months of preparing for surgery, I had to visit with the doctor and take medication.

On April 15, 2008, my daughter had her graduation ceremony for becoming a CNA, and I missed it. I was in the hospital having surgery, but the Lord brought me through it. I spent a few days in the hospital, and then I went home. The house was not up to my standards, so I begin to clean up. The next day I was supposed to see my doctor, and I wound up back in surgery because I was hemorrhaging. The doctor found out where I was bleeding and went in to stop it. So, I was back in the hospital.

I was in the hospital a few days, but I could not rest. The Lord sent my sister-in-law, and she came with all kinds of products to clean my room and help me bathe. Thank you Lord! My room smelled so good until the patient's next door hollered to my sister-in-law, "Can you come and do *my* room?" That night I slept so good.

After being in the hospital for a few days, I was supposed to go home. The doctor came into the room and said, "I can't release you because you caught a staff infection. I need you to stay in the hospital 10 more days so we can treat you and give you medication. I said, "Oh no! Find another way. I'm going home!" So, they fixed me up and sent me home. A nurse came to my house every day to treat me. When May came, I was able to get out of the house to go see my twins graduate from high school. Thank you Lord! It was a journey, but the Lord got my family and me through it. He blessed me to see all of my children graduate from high school.

Stepping Out in Ministry

S ome time passed, and we decided to rent a building
and start our own church. A while back my husband
and I came up with a name for a church while
driving in his big truck. We passed by a church, and
my husband stated, Faith Believer's Church. I said to him, no
Believers by Faith Ministry.

We rented a community center for a few months to hold
services. Then, my sister found a building. We were in that
same building for over seven or eight years. What and
experience we had! There were a lot of sacrifices (like fixing
the building and working up until 1o'clock in the morning),

but we pushed through it. We encouraged ourselves and opened the church.

The Lord blessed us to have everything we needed to open the church. We had people in the neighborhood come sit through the service and ask for prayer. We counseled some people and even gave away clothes and food in front of the church. The Lord blessed, and we had several people to join the ministry.

There were also some lessons that we learned by having the ministry. We learned how to deal with people who would try to take over the church and steal the members. Others were like leeches trying to drain us dry, always wanting us to give but not wanting to work in the ministry. At the same time, we were trying to help those who were coming to learn about the Lord. It was a lot of work, but it's what kept me going. It was comforting to know that I was helping someone, just like God was helping me.

I want my testimony to help and encourage someone that life lessons and the choices you make in your life are not only for you; they are also for the people who are around you. You will have to live with the choices that you make and pass down to your children. This is why the Lord gave me a special scripture, and I have placed it in the front of the church and made cards to pass out to people. Proverbs 3:5-6 states trust in the Lord with all thine heart, and lean not on thine own understanding. In all thy ways acknowledge him, and he shall direct thy paths. Every time I read this scripture, I learn from it. It encourages me and lets me know that I am not alone in this walk of life. There is a God, and he is with me at all times. When I am sick or when I am weak, he is caring for me and healing me. When I am scared, he is protecting me and fighting for me. Once I learned this, things became easy.

I realized that God is the only one you can trust. He is always there for you, and he will never let you down. People are in your life for a season. Some may be leeches, sucking you dry until you want something from them. It may seem like they are always there, and you cannot get rid of them. Sometimes it seems like the people that you love and get good advice from leave you too soon. When these people die or leave you, you are hurt and you just don't understand why they had to go. Only God knows the reason why.

Later in life, I figured out for myself that the memories are extremely important. You have to push to go on and continue to encourage someone else. I thank God for my life here on this earth that he made. He blessed me with a wonderful family that he created so I could see what prayer could do. I was created to listen and do what God says to do in order to see instant results. The choices I made in my life are showing fully to this day, the good and the bad. Through God I am living with it by his grace and mercy. God is with me.

Lessons Learned

I've learned that in this world everything is moving fast. You barely have a chance to enjoy it. You get up, work, take care of your family, sleep and repeat. Thank God for the Holy Spirit that dwells inside of us to help lead and guide us. The Holy Spirit lets us know that we are in this world, but we are not of this world. So, we have a choice to do what the world is offering or to choose the Lord. I choose the Lord because I see what my life is like without him. It is terrible. I see how others live without God, and I want no parts of that.

Growing up as a child, it seemed like life was short. I learned how the adults acted at a young age after my father passed. From then on, my life changed. I realized that in this world there is a battle, and the only way you are going to make it is if you are on the Lord's side.

Going to church when I was coming up helped me a lot. Listening to the speakers and songs and praying on my own helped me a whole lot too! I give all the credit to my Lord and Savior, Jesus Christ, who guided me and answered my prayers of being a good wife and mother. I also prayed about how to take care of a home, a business, and a church. All glory belongs to God and not man for the guidance he gave to me.

Once the lesson has been learned and you have lived it, let it be a testimony to help someone else. Second Timothy 2:12 says that if we suffer with Christ, we will also reign with him. If we deny him, he will deny us before his father in heaven.

I thank God for the opportunity that he is giving me each time I can tell someone how awesome my father is to my love ones and me. That's why I love to see and talk about the goodness of God. I know him to be a miracle worker, a healer, a provider, a counselor, a teacher, and a friend. The list could go on and on.

The Lord will wake you up to intercede for your love ones and people you do not know. I remember times that my husband was in several bad accidents as a truck driver, and the Lord brought him out of each one. There was even a total loss of several trucks, but because of my God, my husband came out of each accident with not a scratch on him. God is an awesome God! Who wouldn't serve a God like that?

The points I want to make are that my God is awesome, and his word is true. He will never leave you. He is always there; just trust him and be obedient. Let him lead you to the path that he has prepared for you.

One thing I can say about David is that he was a fighter. He continued to ask for forgiveness and continued to serve God through his good choices and bad choices.

I know some things are hard to do after you have been hurt by people you love, especially when the people who hurt you are leaders in the church who are still preaching God's word. The Lord may have you to intercede for them and then leave the church. I know firsthand that forgiving is a hard thing to do, but with God nothing is impossible. He can and will do it. Just let God heal you and continue to move on because God has greater inside of you. Just endure like a good soldier, and then keep moving. Remember that the choices that you make affect others.

About the Author

Dana Renee Gibson Monroe was born in Queens, New York and is the second oldest of seven children. She moved to South Carolina as a young girl and experienced many trials and triumphs growing up. After receiving a Child Development associate degree through the Head Start program, she began volunteering at the Economic Opportunity Authority and later became a teacher there. Gaining years of knowledge of working with little ones, Monroe was lead by the Lord to open *Dana's Learning Center* which she still owns and operates today.

In 2007, Dana Monroe endured grave health issues that sent her to the hospital for a long while. During her illness and recuperation, the Lord began to deal with her about writing and sharing her testimony with the world. As a wife, mother, grandmother, entrepreneur, and ministry leader, she is a living witness that the choices you make affect not only you but also those around you.

Made in the USA
Columbia, SC
24 July 2022

63697959R00043